DIGITAL AND INFORMATION LITERACY ™

CITED!
IDENTIFYING CREDIBLE INFORMATION ONLINE
REVISED AND UPDATED

LARRY GERBER

rosen publishing's
rosen central®

New York

Published in 2018 by The Rosen Publishing Group, Inc.
29 East 21st Street, New York, NY 10010

Library of Congress Cataloging-in-Publication Data

Names: Gerber, Larry.
Title: Cited! identifying credible information online / Larry Gerber.
Description: New York : Rosen Central, 2018. | Series: Digital and information literacy | Includes glossary and index. | Audience: Grades 5–8.
Identifiers: ISBN 9781499439052 (library bound) | ISBN 9781499439038 (pbk.) | ISBN 9781499439045 (6 pack)
Subjects: LCSH: Internet research—Juvenile literature. | Internet searching—Juvenile literature. | Computer network resources—Evaluation—Juvenile literature. | Electronic information resource literacy–Juvenile literature.
Classification: LCC ZA4228.G47 2018 | DDC 001.4′202854678—dc23

Manufactured in China

CONTENTS

INTRODUCTION

With so much of human knowledge available at one's fingertips at any time, it is difficult to conceive of a time when research was conducted without the internet to rely on. More than twenty years ago, certain facts or data that now take seconds to uncover sometimes took hours of digging through physical books and records. Any decent researcher would have to plan for a trip to one or more libraries to find books and archived magazines, newspapers, and academic journals.

Help from librarians was even more crucial in finding the right sources. But doing the research itself meant hours of flipping pages and taking notes, mostly by hand before word processing software became the way most students did it.

Even more time-consuming and difficult was the search for audio and video recordings—for example, of historical events. Physical copies on old formats like VHS tape, or even reels of film, had to be located and then obtained, or at least tracked down to request access to them.

Another convenient process we take for granted these days was finding photographs, or at least usable copies of them. Photos and audiovisual sources were both stored in many different places, and whole teams of professionals were needed to catalogue and track their use. That was true if good records existed to begin with. In many cases, even historical

Getting information—whether in print or online, in the library or elsewhere—is part of the hard work, and joy, of research.

documents were stored in random and forgotten archives. Some disappeared or degraded with age.

What a difference a few decades makes. The internet has unlocked a world of research possibilities for casual aficionados, and more important, for serious researchers of all ages. The great news is that information is ever more plentiful and easy to access. Digital records of many important sources, images, documents, films, and more exist in many different networks and are trackable across millions of websites.

But information does not equal fact, nor does it equal "the truth." Anyone familiar with current events can tell that there are many conflicting ideas and ideologies online, and it is sometimes very difficult to figure out what agendas information sources suggest. Even reputable news organizations get their stories wrong. Politicians, academics, journalists, celebrities, and others all have their own opinions, agendas, and interests.

Finding facts and credible information and data in an ocean of written and visual content online is something all good researchers need to master. How do researchers distinguish between propaganda and news, and determine what information is relevant to research topics they are interested in? What are the right ways to cite sources? Let's get started in figuring out how to cite credible information online.

→ **Chapter 1**

Digging Up the Truth

The sources we use in research include ones across a whole variety of media. These sources provide us with information. A piece of information that we know to be true is a fact. But what do we really mean by media and sources?

The word "media" is merely the plural of medium. Television is one medium. Books are another. The internet may be considered an entirely different medium, even if sometimes it includes and delivers several media together (including words, video, podcasts, and more). In this sense, it can even be considered a type of super-media. Newspapers and film are two more types. Even a handwritten note or a smartphone are considered media, since they both deliver information in some way.

Sources are the starting points of information. Sources can be things, but they are usually people or groups of people. When a friend phones to say the party starts at 8:00 p.m., the medium is the phone; the source is the friend.

If we want to find the current US population, the medium is the internet; the source is the US Census Bureau.

While many print-based media, like newspapers, are well established and seem credible, researchers must remember that all sources must be properly vetted.

The most important quality of a source is credibility. When we say a source is credible, we mean that we can believe the source's information.

To judge credibility, we need to be clear about the difference between sources and media. If someone asks, "Where did the information come from?" they're asking for the source. Saying "I saw it on TV" isn't an answer. Television is a medium, not a source.

The distinction is important because we use the internet to tap into a wide variety of media to find sources. It helps to keep in mind the difference between web pages and other material we find on the web. Web pages are designed and written specifically for internet users. But we can also use the internet to access pages of magazines, newspapers, books, video, and audio files.

Credible sources in all media usually tell us their sources of information so we can check them for accuracy.

File   Edit   View   Favorites   Tools   Help

WHAT'S CREDIBLE

What's Credible?

Here's an example of the difference between scholarly content and other types of media material that we find on the web. Do a Google search for "causes of wars." The top result will probably be a Wikipedia page. Check it out. No authors are listed. Sometimes sources are cited, but a few sections neglect to say where the information came from.

Now do the same search using Google Scholar. There's a list of books and papers. Most have been reviewed by experts, fact-checked, and edited. The author's names are usually right at the top. The entries cite sources for the facts they use. The Wikipedia entry is a regular web page. Most of the Google Scholar results are pages that been published elsewhere as well as on the web.

Which seems to be the most credible?

Two Types of Sources

There are two main types of source: primary and secondary. Primary sources give us firsthand information. People involved in an accident are primary sources of information about the accident. So are people who saw the accident. Primary sources are often in the best position to know what happened.

Autobiographies—books written by people about themselves—are primary sources. So are diaries. Experts can be primary sources. People like doctors and scientists who have studied something for years can give us firsthand information about it. Some primary sources aren't people. Photos,

This 1820 painting, *The Surrender of Cornwallis at Yorktown* by John Trumbull, depicting the British general's surrender that ended the American Revolution, can be considered a secondary source.

paintings, coins, statues, pottery, and other artifacts can tell researchers a lot about the times when they were created.

In other words, primary sources usually refer to people and documents that can mostly be counted on. But, like people involved in an accident, people who are primary sources may not always be sure which facts are the most important. Secondary sources take their facts from primary sources. They give us the benefit of analysis and perspective. Secondary sources include reference books, articles, nonfiction books, and television programs. Biographies—books written about people by others—are secondary sources.

Journalists are common secondary sources. Reporters don't always witness the events they report, but they usually talk to people who did. People who report news for a living are often credible because they have been trained for their jobs, and their livelihood depends on their credibility. Most of their reporting can be checked for accuracy against other news stories. Print reporting usually has more detail than reporting on radio and television.

The internet has made new kinds of reporting possible. People who haven't been trained as journalists write blogs and articles and offer commentary on more open-ended forums like Twitter and other social media networks. Since there are millions of potential "citizen journalists," many fill in information gaps in places where there are few or no regular journalists. They may find information that regular journalists cannot access.

But those conditions also make it hard to confirm information. Sometimes it's impossible to know who bloggers and tweeters are. So it's usually best to be careful about using such sources. We can't judge whether a source is credible if we don't know who it is. Many—but by no means all—Twitter users who are also writers, reporters, and scholars have a blue checkmark next to their handles, indicating they are verified users. Trusted sources like these may also have blogs and other periodic content postings, whether they are hosted on a well known media entity's site, or independently. Those who disclose their identities plainly are often more likely to provide reliable content.

One of the first things we need to determine about a source is whether he, she, or it is qualified to give us accurate information: Is the source in a position to know the facts?

Bias: Know It When You See It

When something is biased, that means it is slanted or prejudiced. Everyone has a point of view, and everyone presents information from that viewpoint. The reasons may be understandable. A newspaper may seem biased by printing a very short story about a very important topic. Readers may think the story should be longer, when the editor simply didn't have enough space that day.

No one, not even the best source, can be entirely free of bias. We all have our points of view, our likes and dislikes. Professional reporters are taught to watch out for their personal biases and keep them out of their reporting as much as possible. But some bias is intentional. Some sources want us to see things as they do. They leave out important facts. They treat trivial facts as important. Biased sources usually don't tell us why they want to slant the information.

When we suspect bias, we should ask ourselves certain questions. Is my source emphasizing some facts and playing down others? Why? How could the source benefit by slanting the information?

The best way to detect bias is to check the source against other sources. It is usually the only way. That's why researchers try to have at least two sources for every piece of information. When it comes to sources, more is better. Using multiple sources to test for credibility is a two-part job. The first part is finding out what others say about the source. Is he a Nobel Prize scholar? A veteran reporter? A notorious practical joker?

If the source is credible, go on to step two: Do others agree with the information? Do other sources say something slightly different? Is it entirely different? For most topics, there are plenty of sources available on the internet or in the library. With practice, bias becomes easier to spot.

MYTHS & FACTS

MYTH Sites like Wikipedia are completely untrustworthy.

FACT There are many thousands of articles on Wikipedia that are mostly or completely fact based and accurate. However, there is no guarantee that articles on any given topic will be based on properly vetted research.

MYTH You can pretty much believe everything you read in well-known newspapers or magazines.

FACT Even respected and well-known news outlets can get a story wrong or mistakenly spread propaganda or even lies. It is up to researchers and critical readers and thinkers to corroborate bits of news and information from one source with those from other sources.

MYTH If a site looks and seems professional, it probably publishes trustworthy content.

FACT The accuracy or trustworthiness of a site's content should always require a second opinion or look. Well-designed or professional-looking sites may have very serious biases or viewpoints skewed toward particular agendas.

Chapter 2

Four Kinds of Questionable Facts

I f we know what misinformation, propaganda, or biased content look like, we can usually take steps to avoid it, or at least use it responsibly. Even false information, or highly opinionated news disguised as objective fact, can tell us things we need to know. First, however, consider four different ways one might be fooled.

Fact or Opinion?

Facts are the basis of research because facts can be tested to determine whether they're true or false. Opinion is a problem for researchers because it's never true or false. If we can prove something, it isn't an opinion. It's a fact. Researchers need to be on the lookout for opinion disguised as fact. Everybody's entitled to an opinion. But credible sources let us know clearly when they're giving us their opinion. Reliable newspapers, for example, put opinion columns and letters on their editorial page, not their news pages.

Some sources aren't so reliable. They are so sure about their opinion that they really believe it's fact. And some people don't know the difference.

In the 2000s, many young TV viewers turned to satirical news shows—like those of comedian broadcasters Stephen Colbert (*left*) and Jon Stewart (*right*). These viewers mistrusted more official sources, which they felt had their own biases.

When we're confused about the difference between fact and opinion, a good test question is: Who says? Sources who state facts should have no trouble saying where they got the information. Look out for phrases like "Everybody knows . . ." and "It's obvious that . . ." Those are signals that the next phrase might be opinion disguised as fact.

Detecting Propaganda

Propaganda is information that promotes a certain point of view. While propaganda isn't always false, per se, it's always biased. There are several common varieties. Much of the propaganda we see is advertising. People selling products or services understandably present them in the best possible light. Advertising is everywhere in media. Newspapers, magazine, some blogs, and broadcast programs all earn money by advertising. Credible media sources keep their ads and their factual information clearly separated.

A lot of propaganda is political. People looking for votes and support often make biased statements to promote their ideas. Before accepting "facts" from a politician or political party, it helps to compare an opposing view.

A bird landing on the podium of 2016 presidential candidate and US senator from Vermont Bernie Sanders electrified his audience. As exciting as certain events may be, researchers must divorce their feelings from their research and observations.

Personal propaganda has flourished with the internet. People publish their information and comments on the web for lots of reasons—anything from finding jobs to finding companionship. Most people want to look good, so their information is often biased. And it's often hard to check.

Social propaganda promotes all sorts of causes, and many of them are great causes. There are groups that hope to combat climate change, raise money for hungry children, and engage in other causes. But even when the cause it worthy, it's unlikely that these sources will present information that may potentially hurt their cause.

Propaganda may contain facts that are accurate and fair to use in research. But it seldom shows the whole picture. It's often only one side of an argument. Good researchers find opposing points of view for balance. One way to detect propaganda is to ask: Why is the source presenting this information? People who publish propaganda have a reason for going to all the trouble. Knowing the reason can help us sort out the facts.

Disinformation or Misinformation

Everybody makes mistakes, even sources with the best of intentions. Honest mistakes are misinformation. People can be wrong and still believe they're perfectly correct. That's because we all tend to see things in different ways.

There's an old story often told by police officers and reporters: Five people witness a traffic accident. All five give different versions of what happened. The story illustrates how memory isn't always reliable.

Autobiographers sometimes write their life stories years after the events they describe. Historians treat such accounts with great care because they know that people's memories can play tricks. When mistakes are made on purpose, we call it disinformation. It's not always bad. Some websites publish hilarious news satires. People use Photoshop to alter pictures for the same kind of laughs. It can all be funny as long as we know it isn't real.

But disinformation can be downright evil. Dictators like Hitler and Stalin commanded huge propaganda organizations that doctored pictures

Police and other emergency responders arrive at the scene of an incident and interview witnesses, many of whom may offer slightly varying accounts of what occurred.

and spread lies about political enemies and minorities. Millions died because people believed their vicious disinformation.

Governments are especially tempted to spread disinformation during wartime. They may compare their enemies to animals or accuse them of atrocities in order to make their own populations more willing to fight. Rumor and gossip are two other types of disinformation. Unethical media use rumor and gossip to attract readers and advertisers. In addition, there are always a few people who simply don't know and don't care. They will put bad information online just because they can.

File   Edit   View   Favorites   Tools   Help

 TESTING PHONY FACTS

Testing Phony Facts

Sometimes we can spot phony facts just by looking at them. When we're not sure, a two-part test may help.

1. Do a web search using the source's name. What do others say about him, her, or it? What are the source's qualifications? What does the source do for a living? Does the source have anything to gain by slanting the information?
2. Find material similar to the source's by doing a search using key phrases from the source's material. Does the new material agree? Has anybody else used the source's material?

If the source fails either part of the test, dump it and move on. Check the comparison material from step two for possible new sources.

Keeping an Eye Out

How can we tell phony "facts" from real ones? Remember to ask: Who says? Reliable sources give attribution for things they say—they make it a point to let us know where the information came from so we can check it for ourselves. Attribution is a source's way of telling us: "I didn't make this up." If there's no attribution in the source material, look out!

Exaggeration and innuendo are also warning signs. Another word for exaggeration is "hyperbole," or "hype." Some news organizations hype stories and facts to make them seem more important than they really are. Innuendo means saying something without really putting it in words. We see examples in news stories that ask questions without answering them:

"Is this man a murderer?" If he is, the headline should say so. Otherwise, it shouldn't be implied.

"Little" mistakes in writing and punctuation can be another sign of source trouble. We know everybody makes mistakes, but if a source is careless with spelling and grammar, we have to wonder how careful the source is with facts.

Emotional and inflammatory language is a strong indicator of bias. Racial slurs and hate speech are extreme examples. Other kinds of emotional language appeal to our pity, envy, pride, or other feelings rather than our thinking.

Emotional language can be deceiving. Imagine discovering a charity soliciting online declaring, "HelpKidsInc desperately needs your contribution to help sick children around the world!" Does it sound like HelpKidsInc could be a worthy cause? Absolutely. Who wouldn't want to help sick kids? But take a closer look. Does it say that HelpKidsInc has actually helped any children?

Chapter 3

What's Relevant and What's Not?

Beyond the veracity, or truth, of information and content found online, shrewd scholars must ask themselves about relevance. Is it true or trustworthy? If so, their next questions about the information should be, "Is it relevant?" "Does this information matter?" "What does it have to do with my research subject?"

Getting Topical

New content is posted online every second, but not all of it is new. It includes content that is literally hundreds of years old. Does it matter how old information is? It depends on one's research subject. For example, those writing about social networks online might uncover a statistic that Tumblr has more users than Instagram. The source of the statistic is thought to be generally reliable. The information is reliable, too. Or is it? A deeper dig into online news sites might reveal that in 2017 Instagram actually had more users than Tumblr. A researcher must make sure his or her information is up to date.

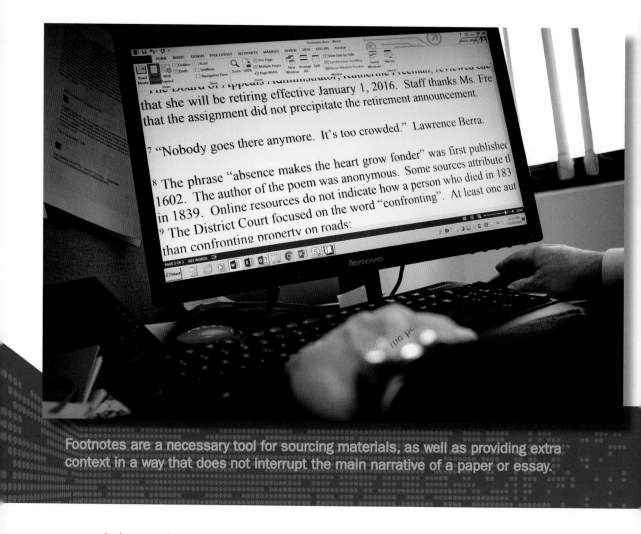

Footnotes are a necessary tool for sourcing materials, as well as providing extra context in a way that does not interrupt the main narrative of a paper or essay.

Subjects that people read about, talk about, and write about every day are known as topical subjects. They include anything that's in the news and just about anything to do with the internet.

For topical subjects, the most recent information is vital. Some subjects aren't so time sensitive. Historians and scientists are constantly doing new work. And good researchers are always checking to see what's new. But basic facts about subjects like Roman emperor Julius Caesar or the human digestive system rarely change daily.

Does It Really Matter?

The great majority of news in the United States comes to us through commercial, for-profit media. More viewers or readers equal more ads and more money. It is thus natural for news organizations, online and off, as well as television and radio stations to make their news seem important.

Sensationalism is a way of making information seem more important than it really is. For example, it is obvious that crimes like murder and kidnapping get the public's attention. Reading the headlines and feeling the emotions they arouse might make readers believe that crime is getting out of hand. In fact, the US Justice Department says violent crime has been declining for the past twenty-five years. The reporting on each individual crime may be perfectly accurate, but sensationalism can give us a false idea of the bigger picture.

File   Edit   View   Favorites   Tools   Help

ARE THEY SERIOUS?

Are They Serious?

Sometimes the look of web pages can provide clues as to the quality of its information. Some warning signs may include odd backgrounds or wallpaper, a mix of too many strange fonts or typefaces, juvenile icons or emojis, strange links that seem that they will launch pop-ups, and more. Any or all of the above should raise one's alarms. There's nothing wrong with interesting graphic elements. And facts don't have to look dull. But it's more important that the page be functional: Does it have useful information? Do the links work? Do the links connect to credible sources? Do the links connect to information about the site?

Glamour and celebrity also get attention and sell ads. Provocative pictures may be fun to look at and celebrities fun to read about. But keep the research topic in mind. If you are covering celebrity or fashion in some way or researching a person's biography, these subjects are relevant. If not, they are probably best avoided. Glamour and trends are just other forms of sensationalism.

Format can also trick people. Many websites and other media use repetitive formatting, meaning they use the same logos, music, studio sets, or typefaces repeatedly. Radio and TV personalities often repeat themselves. Formatting is a way of making the presentation familiar. And familiar things naturally seem more credible, whether or not they really are.

Saying Less with More

All kinds of experts and specialists, from scientists to sports announcers, have special vocabularies and ways of speaking. Academics and experts are known for using advanced vocabulary and complex sentence constructions. Specialized words that apply to a certain field are sometimes known as jargon.

Jargon helps specialists communicate among themselves, but it's not always a good way to communicate with others. Such material often sounds terribly official and important, like something we might need in our research. Some people overuse jargon to sound like experts.

Specialists often do need jargon to convey important ideas. Researchers may often have to sort out tough passages. Elaborate wording can be a cover, however—or a distraction from—substandard ideas or arguments. Good writers can communicate something important in language that nearly everybody can understand.

Graphs and charts are great ways to convey complicated information. But graphics should be clear, too, and relevant. Writers of long reports are sometimes tempted to throw in graphics just to break up pages of print. Graphics can make reports look more "factual" without adding much information.

A good speaker might be able to guide an audience through many different images at once, but it is usually best to keep presentation visuals simple and easy to follow.

Message over Medium

Researchers can be easily misled by irrelevant material. Casual readers and watchers, and researchers as well, can be influenced not only by the information they get through a medium but by the medium itself.

Humans use different parts of the brain to process what they read, hear, and see on screens or in photos. Let's say one person sees a speech online or on television. Another hears it on a podcast or on the radio, and another reads it to himself. Each person is likely to have different ideas

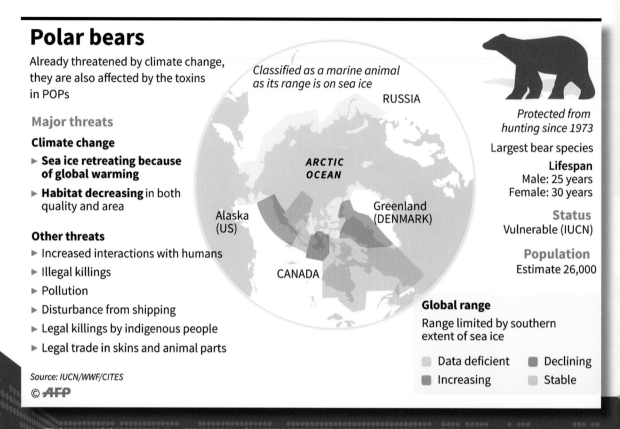

Polar bears

Already threatened by climate change, they are also affected by the toxins in POPs

Major threats

Climate change

▶ **Sea ice retreating because of global warming**

▶ **Habitat decreasing** in both quality and area

Other threats

▶ Increased interactions with humans

▶ Illegal killings

▶ Pollution

▶ Disturbance from shipping

▶ Legal killings by indigenous people

▶ Legal trade in skins and animal parts

Source: IUCN/WWF/CITES

© *AFP*

Classified as a marine animal as its range is on sea ice

RUSSIA

ARCTIC OCEAN

Greenland (DENMARK)

Alaska (US)

CANADA

Protected from hunting since 1973

Largest bear species

Lifespan
Male: 25 years
Female: 30 years

Status
Vulnerable (IUCN)

Population
Estimate 26,000

Global range

Range limited by southern extent of sea ice

▢ Data deficient   ▢ Declining
▢ Increasing   ▢ Stable

This graphic generally succeeds in showing information about climate change and animal habitats with a simple and easy-to-follow design.

about the speech and about what parts of it are important. On-screen, the speaker may smile and gesture. Viewers will be influenced just by the way he or she looks. That won't affect radio or podcast listeners, but they will be influenced by the speaker's pauses and tone of voice.

Do those things matter for our research? They might, if our topic is the speaker. It's a good idea to read the speech for ourselves. Getting material in writing not only helps eliminate mistakes, it helps us judge the importance of the material—as opposed to the way the material is presented.

Chapter 4

Using Sources Responsibly

n the internet age, the sources for any particular set of statistics, quotes, or other bits of information can often be complicated and fuzzy. Beyond the credibility and relevance of information and data, modern researchers must also consider how they can use these things and how to credit and cite sources. There are many images and bits of text online that are free to use, but almost anything out there needs to be credited to some person, organization, or website.

Avoiding Plagiarism

Plagiarism means taking somebody else's words or ideas and passing them off as our own without giving credit to the source. It is a type of theft and an open secret that people have been doing it since the invention of writing itself.

Professional researchers and respected writers, some with advanced degrees and years of experience, have lost their jobs and their reputations because of plagiarism. Sometimes they lose money, too. Courts can impose

Photocopying or scanning pages from books that one may be unable to borrow or buy is usually a better alternative to taking notes that may be tougher to review later than printed text.

fines for violations of copyright laws, which protect much written material, works of art, music, and computer programs. For students, plagiarism results in failing grades. In some cases, people are kicked out of school.

Getting caught is easier than it might seem. Websites and apps—some offered via subscriptions to educators, schools, and publishers—provide online and academic search engines designed for teachers to check for plagiarized material. Tracking down stolen research is pretty simple even without a special search engine. Just put a phrase into quotation marks on

Google—for example, try "The only thing we have to fear is fear itself"—and see what comes up.

The main victims of plagiarism are the ones who do it. A big part of research is learning things for oneself and learning how to communicate acquired knowledge. Research isn't as difficult or complicated as it's often made out to be. Most researchers, especially students, are expected to use the work of others. But they're expected to use it fairly and correctly. It's easy to avoid plagiarism. The key is attribution: naming our sources of information and giving credit where it is due.

Even if one's entire paper quotes extensively from other sources, that is completely fine—as long as the researcher includes the proper attributions and citations. Plagiarism can just as easily occur accidentally as

Native American author Sherman Alexie speaks during Indigenous People's Day in October 2016 in Seattle, Washington. Alexie himself once accused another author, Tim Barrus, of stealing some of his work.

intentionally. This is especially true if someone is in a big hurry to meet a deadline and ends up doing a great deal of research in a short amount of time. Various sources can get mixed up in even capable researchers' heads. If they do not take good notes, they may come across things they have jotted down and even mistake them for their own original insights. They then include these things without citing the sources, opening a can of worms of potential trouble.

Another reason plagiarism is so controversial and widespread now is that it is so easy to retrieve information with a mouse click or screen

File   Edit   View   Favorites   Tools   Help

RECORDING SOURCE INFORMATION

Recording Source Information

The copy-and-paste function of computers and other devices is a great way to save source material. It's also a good idea to save attribution material at the same time. Professional researchers usually keep the following items so they can use them when it's time to cite their sources.

1. The name of the source
2. The name of the media carrying the information: titles of books, magazines, newspapers, radio or TV programs, websites, etc.
3. URL addresses for internet material
4. The date the material was published or posted
5. The date it was accessed, if it came from an online source. This can be important because web pages sometimes disappear.

Student researchers don't always have to provide all those items in their research papers, but they can come in very handy if they're kept on file.

swipe. The pressure to succeed can even tempt students to enlist the services of online "paper mills." These services offer to write papers for free, sometimes according to a student's needs, sometimes offering ready-made, prewritten ones. Whatever the pressure on students, they should avoid risking their academic reputation and future—and even expulsion at the college level—by getting mixed up in a situation that could spell big trouble if discovered.

Attribution Pointers

Some assignments require attribution in footnotes or endnotes, particularly for college-level work and beyond. Instructors will usually say what format to use and how much information should be given.

But certain types of information should always be attributed to a source. They are:

- Direct quotations
- Paraphrased ideas
- Other ideas taken from a source
- Statistics and other data provided by a source

Quoted Material

Quotations are a source's exact words. They should always go inside quotation marks, and the source should be cited directly before or after the quotation. Here's a made-up example:

> "The studies that we have conducted over the past ten years show that drivers between the ages of 16 and 19 react more quickly than drivers over 50 years of age," said Dr. Michelle Richards of the National Auto Safety Administration.

Plagiarism is a serious matter. Those who get caught doing it are lucky if the worst that happens is they get a stern lecture from a professor or academic advisor. More serious repercussions can include expulsion from school and ruining one's career.

Paraphrased Material

Paraphrases are similar to quotations, but they don't use the source's exact words. We often paraphrase to shorten direct quotations or make them clearer. Paraphrases don't go inside quotation marks. The source should be cited directly before or after the paraphrase. Take this example: "Studies over the past ten years show that teenage drivers have quicker reactions than drivers over 50, according to Dr. Michelle Richards of the National Auto Safety Administration."

Idea Attribution

We should attribute ideas that aren't our own, even when we're not quoting or paraphrasing. Example: "The National Auto Safety Administration says teenage drivers react faster than older drivers." Ideas that are well known and generally accepted don't need attribution. One example might be, "Alcohol can slow a driver's reactions." If there's any doubt about whether an idea should be attributed, it's a good idea to ask the person who assigned the research.

Charts, Graphs, and Statistics

Let's say that we find a big chart giving all kinds of statistics on driver reaction times on the website of the (made-up) National Auto Safety Administration. We might take out the information we need and present it like this:

Driver age	Average driver reaction time
16	0.5 seconds
50	1.5 seconds

Source: National Auto Safety Administration

If we put the figures in written text, the information still needs to be attributed. For instance, "The average reaction time for 16-year-old drivers is one-half second, compared with 1.5 seconds for 50-year-olds, according to the National Auto Safety Administration."

Chapter 5

Source Detectives

When it comes to criminal acts, professionals known as investigators gather clues to form a picture of what probably happened at a crime scene. Researchers have to be equally diligent about their various sources, looking at them closely, weighing one against others, and responding to new information.

A Closer Look at Online Sources

The URL, or uniform resource locator, is the line of letters and numbers that usually begins with h t t p in the browser's address space. URLs can reveal several things about the page on the screen. Top-level domain (TLD) designations are three-letter codes. The most familiar is probably ".com." TLDs often tell us what kind of organization is hosting the page. Colleges and universities use ".edu." Governments in the United States use ".gov" and can be good sources of official information.

Several years ago, ".com" was set aside for commercial businesses, ".org" for nonprofit and charity groups, and ".net" for internet service

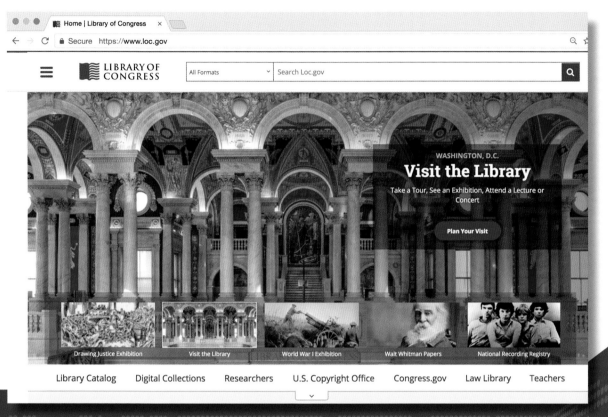

The Library of Congress, including its vast collection of online media, images, and documents, is a fantastic and free resource for student researchers. Many of its archival images can be used freely, as long as credit is given.

providers. Now, just about anyone can use one of those designations. You will notice that nowadays there seem to newer ones every day.

Source organizations usually say something about themselves on their websites. Look for links at the top, bottom, or edges of the page that say things like "About Us," "Information," or "Mission Statement."

Most sites have a Contacts link that shows officers in the organization and says how to get more information. There may also be a Comments section, for what it's worth. Look for a date, often at the bottom of the page, that says when the page was last updated.

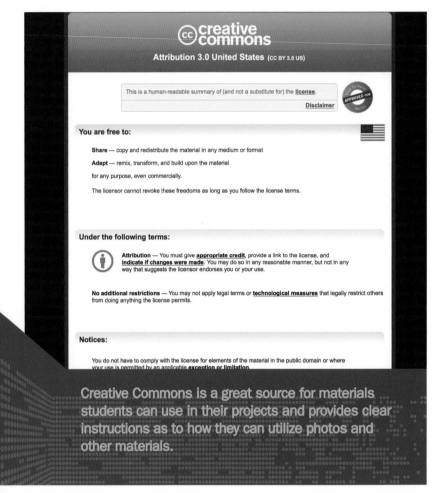

Creative Commons is a great source for materials students can use in their projects and provides clear instructions as to how they can utilize photos and other materials.

Some sites post conditions for use of their material. Read them before using. For student use, educational sites usually ask only that they be credited.

Websites that specialize in information about other sites can be handy evaluation tools. They show who owns a site, what kind of information it handles, and how much traffic it has. They may also say how many other sites link to it and how users rate its quality.

Articles, Posts, and Online and Print Materials

Blogs come in all shapes and sizes, but credible blogs always identify the sources of their information. Posting dates should be easy to find. Many bloggers also post links to their biographies so readers can judge their qualifications. Sometimes it may be necessary to do a search on an individual blogger's name to find qualifications. If no sources, posting dates, or qualifications are given anywhere, it's probably time to find another source.

Books, whether physical ones or e-books, usually have their printing dates on one of the very first pages. If the book has been updated, that will usually be mentioned in an editor's note or foreword. Author information is usually on the book jacket or cover, or on one of the pages just before or after the main text.

Most newspapers and magazines put the date of their publication on the front page or cover. Online articles usually have most material dated and often mark whether something was updated or corrected after that, too. Look for writers' names at the top or the bottom of each article. If the writer works for the publication, there may not be a separate biography. But most publications have staff information on their websites. Librarians can usually tell us a lot about source publications. For online information, search "newspaper directories" or "magazine directories."

TEN GREAT QUESTIONS

TO ASK A RESEARCH LIBRARIAN

1 What's a reliable place to find sources of information about my research topic?

2 Who or what is the best primary source for that information?

3 What's the source's purpose in publishing the information?

4 Does the source have a special point of view?

5 Where can I find out what others think about that source?

6 Where can I find other points of view about the information?

7 How old is the information?

8 What are the best secondary sources for the information about my subject?

9 Do any of the sources have reason to be biased?

10 Is there any reason why this information shouldn't be used in my research paper?

GLOSSARY

argument In logic, a series of statements leading to a conclusion.

attribution Identifying an information source in a research paper or essay, either within the text, in a footnote, or through another format.

bias The way a source's point of view affects the way a source presents information. Sources aren't always conscious of their biases.

conclusion The result of a logical argument, or the outcome of research.

credibility The quality of being trusted and believed in.

deductive argument A series of statements leading to a conclusion that must be true if the statements are true.

disinformation Material that isn't true, and is known by the source to be untrue and disseminated anyway.

facts Bits of information that can be proven, verified, or agreed upon.

fallacy A mistaken logical argument.

format Repetition in the way information is presented in order to make the information seem familiar and credible.

hyperbole Exaggeration used to influence readers or viewers, also known as hype.

inductive argument A series of statements leading to a conclusion that is probably true if the statements are true.

information What sources say or show; words, pictures, data, and other material that we can examine to find facts.

innuendo Leaving out facts but implying a conclusion; letting readers or viewers draw conclusions from things that aren't stated.

misinformation Mistaken information; material that isn't true, although the source may believe it's true.

opinion An idea that someone thinks or believes; a statement that can't be proven true or false.

plagiarism Using a source's words or ideas without giving credit to the source, whether or not one does it maliciously.

propaganda Biased information that's intended to persuade readers, listeners, or viewers to do certain things or think in certain ways.

publish To make information public; to be a source of information.

sensationalism A form of hyperbole, or exaggeration, that often distorts facts, usually to get clicks or other attention from readers or viewers.

source An origin point of information, knowledge, or data, it can include people, groups of people, artifacts, and texts like books and articles.

TLD Top-level domain; the three-letter domain code after the server designation in most URLs (".com," ".edu," etc.).

URL Stands for "uniform resource locator" and refers to a web page's internet address.

FOR MORE INFORMATION

Center for Media Literacy
22603 Pacific Coast Highway, #472
Malibu, CA 90265
(310) 804-3985
Email: cml@medialit.org
Website: http://www.medialit.org
The Center for Media Literacy promotes and supports media literacy educa-
    tion. It works to help all citizens, especially young people, develop
    critical thinking and media production skills.

J Source: Canadian Journalism Project
117 Peter Street, 3rd Floor
Toronto, ON M5V 2G9
Canada
(416) 955-0630
Website: http://www.j-source.ca
Twitter: @jsource
Facebook: @jsource
The Canadian Journalism Project of the Canadian Journalism Foundation
    promotes excellence in journalism, information, and commentary. Its
    site has news, research, advice, discussion, and other resources,
    including tools for locating sources, tools for ensuring accuracy, and
    tools for web research.

Library of Congress
101 Independence Avenue SE
Washington, DC 20540
(202) 707-5000
Website: http://www.loc.gov/families

Twitter: @librarycongress
Facebook: @libraryofcongress
The Library of Congress is the research arm of Congress and maintains the
    largest library in the world. It also offers vast online resources and
    programs for students.

Media Smarts
205 Catherine Street, Suite 100
Ottawa, ON K2P 1C3
Canada
(613) 224-7721
(800) 896-3342 (in North America)
Email: info@mediasmarts.ca
Website: http://mediasmarts.ca
Twitter: @MediaSmarts
Facebook: @MediaSmarts
Media Smarts promotes critical thinking about the media in young people.
    It produces programs and resources for teachers, parents, and students.

Smithsonian Institution: Museum Studies
PO Box 37012, MRC 508
Washington, DC 20013-7012
(202) 633-5330
Email: learning@si.edu
Website: http://museumstudies.si.edu
Twitter: @smithsonian
Facebook: @smithsonian
The Smithsonian Institution is the world's largest museum complex and

research organization. It sponsors a variety of education programs. Its online encyclopedia has information about arts and design, history and culture, and science and technology.

Young Adult Library Services Association
50 East Huron Street
Chicago, IL 60611
(800) 545-2433, ext. 4390
Email: YALSA@ala.org
Website: http://www.ala.org
Twitter: @yalsa
Facebook: @yalsa
The Young Adult Library Services Association promotes library service for students aged twelve to eighteen. It sponsors Teen Read Week and Teen Tech Week. It has a Teen Top Ten favorite book list and other online book lists for research.

Websites

Because of the changing nature of internet links, Rosen Publishing has developed an online list of websites related to the subject of this book. This site is updated regularly. Please use this link to access this list:

http://www.rosenlinks.com/DIL/Cite

FOR FURTHER READING

Cooper, Sheila, and Rosemary Patton. *Writing Logically, Thinking Critically.* 6th ed. New York, NY: Longman Publishing Group, 2009.

Lester, James D. *Writing Research Papers: A Complete Guide.* 15th ed. New York, NY: Longman Publishing Group, 2014.

Lindeen, Mary. *Smart Online Searching: Doing Digital Research.* Minneapolis, MN: Lerner Publishing, 2016.

Mann, Thomas. *The Oxford Guide to Library Research.* 4th ed. New York, NY: Oxford University Press, 2015.

O'Donnel, Liam, and Michael Deas (illustrator). *Media Meltdown: A Graphic Guide Adventure.* Victoria, BC, Canada: Orca Book Publishers, 2009.

Orr, Tamra. *Extraordinary Research Projects.* London, UK: Franklin Watts, 2008.

Porterfield, Jason. *Conducting Basic and Advanced Searches.* New York, NY: Rosen Publishing, 2011.

Reinking, James A. *Strategies for Successful Writing: A Rhetoric, Research Guide, Reader, and Handbook.* 10th ed. Upper Saddle River, NJ: Prentice Hall, 2014.

Ruschmann, Paul. *Media Bias: Point Counterpoint.* Philadelphia, PA: Chelsea House Publishers, 2006.

Weston, Anthony. *A Rulebook for Arguments.* 4th ed. Indianapolis, IN: Hackett Publishing, 2009.

BIBLIOGRAPHY

Gardiner, Eileen, and Ronald G. Musto. *The Digital Humanities: A Primer for Students and Scholars*. New York, NY: Cambridge University Press, 2015.

Goshert, John Charles. *Entering the Academic Conversation: Strategies for Research Writing*. Upper Saddle River, NJ: Pearson, 2014.

Kies, Daniel. "Using Logic in Composition." Department of English, College of DuPage. December 27, 2008. http://papyr.com/hypertextbooks /comp1/logic.htm.

Lenburg, Jeff. *The Facts on File Guide to Research*. New York, NY: Checkmark Books, 2005.

Modern Language Association of America. *MLA Handbook*. 8th ed. New York, NY: Modern Language Association, 2016.

Rozakis, Laurie, PhD. *Shaum's Quick Guide to Writing Great Research Papers*. New York, NY: McGraw-Hill, 1999.

Smith, Alastair. *The Usborne Guide to Homework on the Internet*. London, UK: Usborne Publishing, 2002.

Taparia, Neal. "Do Your Research, Cite Sources to Be an Effective Writer." *Forbes*, September 23, 2015. http://www.forbes.com/sites /nealtaparia/2015/09/23/backup-your-ideas/#3e55e31e216b.

Turabian, Kate L. *A Manual for Writers of Research Papers, Theses, and Dissertation*. 7th ed. Chicago, IL: University of Chicago Press, 2007.

INDEX

About the Author

Larry Gerber has been doing research in person, in libraries, and on the internet for more than thirty-five years. He had edited newspapers and magazines and is a former Associated Press foreign correspondent and bureau chief. He lives in Los Angeles, where he now does independent writing and editing.

Photo Credits

Cover, p. 1 (left) Antonio Guillem/Shutterstock.com; cover, p. 1 (center left), p. 28 wavebreakmedia/Shutterstock.com; cover, p. 1 (center right and right) dennizn/Shutterstock.com, Syda Productions/Shutterstock.com; p. 5 Randy Faris/Corbis/Getty Images; p. 8 Stefan Wolny/Shutterstock.com; p. 10 DEA Picture Library/De Agostini/Getty Images; p. 15 Brad Barket/Getty Images; p. 16 Natalie Behring/Getty Images; p. 18 Steve Dunwell/Photographer's Choice/Getty Images; p. 22 The Washington Post/Getty Images; p. 25 Thomas Barwick/The Image Bank/Getty Images; p. 26 AFP/Newscom; p. 29 © AP Images; p. 32 Niedring/Drentwett/MITO images/Getty Images; cover and interior pages (pixels) © iStockphoto.com/suprun.

Design: Nicole Russo-Duca; Layout: Raúl Rodriguez; Editor: Phil Wolny; Photo Research: Karen Huang

DATE DUE

PRINTED IN U.S.A.